HEROES
and
SHE-ROES

*Poems of Amazing
and Everyday Heroes*

by

J. Patrick Lewis

illustrations by

Jim Cooke

Dial Books for Young Readers
New York

DIAL BOOKS FOR YOUNG READERS
A division of Penguin Young Readers Group
Published by The Penguin Group
Penguin Group (USA) Inc., 375 Hudson Street, New York, NY 10014, U.S.A.
Penguin Group (Canada), 10 Alcorn Avenue, Toronto, Ontario, Canada M4V 3B2
(a division of Pearson Penguin Canada Inc.)
Penguin Books Ltd, 80 Strand, London WC2R 0RL, England
Penguin Ireland, 25 St. Stephen's Green, Dublin 2, Ireland
(a division of Penguin Books Ltd)
Penguin Books India Pvt Ltd, 11 Community Centre,
Panchsheel Park, New Delhi - 110 017, India
Penguin Group (NZ), Cnr Airborne and Rosedale Roads, Albany, Auckland,
New Zealand (a division of Pearson New Zealand Ltd)
Penguin Books (South Africa) (Pty) Ltd, 24 Sturdee Avenue, Rosebank,
Johannesburg 2196, South Africa
Penguin Books Ltd, Registered Offices: 80 Strand,
London WC2R 0RL, England
Text copyright © 2005 by J. Patrick Lewis
Illustrations copyright © 2005 by Jim Cooke
Designed by Lily Malcom
Text set in Garamond 3
Manufactured in China on acid-free paper
10 9 8 7 6 5 4 3 2 1

Library of Congress Cataloging-in-Publication Data
Lewis, J. Patrick.
Heroes and she-roes : poems of amazing and everyday heroes /
J. Patrick Lewis ; illustrations by Jim Cooke.
p. cm.
Summary: Twenty-one poems celebrate and chronicle the actions of real-life
persons (and one dog) who have performed heroic acts in service of others.
ISBN 0-8037-2925-1
1. Courage—Juvenile poetry. 2. Children's poetry, American.
[1. Heroes—Poetry. 2. Courage—Poetry. 3. American poetry.]
I. Cooke, Jim, date, ill. II. Title.
PS3562.E9465H47 2005
811'.54—dc21   2003009239

The art was created using oil
paint on illustration board.

For Bernie and Bob Donaldson
—J.P.L.

To my family, and M.S.
—J.C.

Give thanks to the he- and she-roes
Who will turn upon a dime
When occasion calls for action—
And be there in half the time.

Roll red carpets out for she-roes
And to heroes raise a toast
For extraordinary courage—
Yet you'll never hear them boast.

Lend your hand to he- and she-roes,
To the valiant and the brave,
To those simple people known by
Two simple words: *They gave*.

THE SEEKER

Helen Keller
Author, 1880–1968

My life is such
That every word
I love to touch
I wish I heard.

My fingers clutch
My teacher's hand—
There is so much
To understand.

Such needful crumbs
Excite my soul—
Words taken from
Her finger bowl.

By rule of thumb
I learn to see
And overcome
Adversity.

Helen Adams Keller fell ill at nineteen
months of age, and was left blind and
deaf. A remarkable teacher, Anne
Sullivan, taught Helen to finger-spell.
Helen went on to enter Radcliffe College
and then toured the world sharing her
experiences and encouraging those with
disabilities and advocates for the disabled.
Her written legacy of her life and struggles
continues to inspire and transform lives.

THE ELEMENTARY SCHOOL TEACHER

A teacher is a person
Unafraid
To get the third degree
From Second Grade!

*Teachers are pathfinders, guides,
truth-seekers, champions, role models,
and guardians. Some of the greatest
heroes and she-roes can be found in
classrooms.*

THE EXPLORERS

Meriwether Lewis and William Clark
U.S. Expedition, Pacific Northwest
1804–1806

Mr. Lewis and Mr. Clark
     Saw many, many bears
In very, very scary woods
     In many, many lairs.
The lonesome nights along the trail
     Were very, very dark,
But darker still if bears had trailed
     Mr. Lewis and Mr. Clark.

The Lewis and Clark Expedition of 1804–1806
covered over 8,000 North American land miles.
Facing tremendous hardships, they managed to
provide crucial knowledge about the continent,
including the first scientific descriptions of many
species. Due in some part to the path they forged,
the United States was able to become a
transcontinental nation.

THE UNKNOWN REBEL

Tiananmen Square, Beijing, China
June 5, 1989

The rulers were in hiding,
The day darkened with shame.
The Square would flood with students' blood
Till a man without a name

Appeared from out of nowhere
With nothing on his mind
But to stop the clank of a Chinese tank
That rattled humankind.

Suppose we call him Courage,
Defiance-to-the-Bone,
The symbol of a cut above,
The One Who Stood Alone.

In 1989 a young man who was part of a student-led demonstration for democracy in China, stood and faced a tank in Tiananmen Square—an unprecedented act of defiance and protest within that country. Hundreds of people were killed that day. A passerby dragged the young hero to safety—and oblivion. What ultimately became of him is unknown.

THE WONDER DOG

Togo
Alaska, 1925

Oh, when Togo took off running
With a plucky sled and cunning,
That brave Wonder Dog was stunning—
It was 52° below!

And I'll tell you what he did, he
Relayed his sled dog committee
Many miles towards the city
Through the frozen wastes of snow.

Togo showed 'em how to roam
To save sickly kids at home,
Mushing medicine from Anchorage
Across the ice to Nome.

It's a shaggy-doggy story—
Togo running west to glory,
And it ended hunky-dory
For those children long ago.

In 1925 an outbreak of diphtheria threatened the lives of thousands of children. Racing over 674 frozen miles, sled dogs brought lifesaving medicine. The forgotten hero was Togo, the lead dog of the first and by far the longest leg of the race, some 260 miles.

THE LITTLE ANGEL OF COLOMBIA

Albeiro Vargas
b. June 7, 1979, Colombia, South America

At five Albeiro fed an *abuelita*—
        grandma joyful.
At six he bathed an *abuelito*—
        grandpa found new laughter.
At seven he stole stale bread
        for abuelitos to grow stronger.
At eight he asked the other villagers
        if they would join him.
At nine he built a company,
        their specialty, compassion—
Street urchins like Albeiro,
        "Guardian Angels" on a mission.
French television caught him,
        caught his fever pitch on camera.
At twelve he was adopted by
        the French, who got the message:
Poverty was crushing far too many
        in his country.
Donations fell like petals
        from the flowers in a garden.
Today he tends the Elders' Village,
        home to abuelitos.

While still a young boy Albeiro Vargas organized other
children to join him in caring for the sick and elderly
poor of their community. He and his "Guardian Angels"
continue their work today.

THE PEACEMAKER

Mohandas Gandhi
Leader of India, 1869–1948

My life would end
As it began
Beside a friend,
My fellow man.

With his deep commitment to holiness, civil disobedience, and passive resistance, Gandhi helped bring independent rule to India. Prime Minister Nehru, in telling India of Gandhi's assassination, called him: "The light that has illumined this country . . . and a thousand years later that light will still be seen . . . and the world will see it and it will give solace to innumerable hearts." So great is Gandhi's influence that he inspired nonviolent movements worldwide, notably in the U.S. under Martin Luther King Jr., and in South Africa under Nelson Mandela.

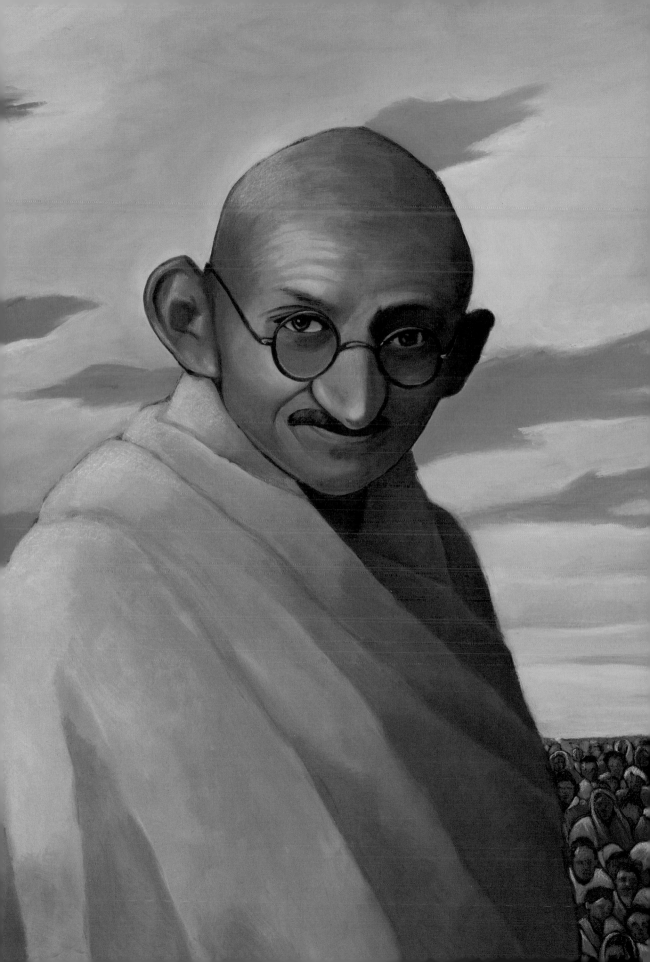

THE FIREFIGHTER

He climbed the stair
To reach the fire
That brought him there,
And climbing higher

Into the smoke
And rubble dust,
Began to choke
Somewhere he must

Have heard the cry.
A person wept,
And driven by
The vow he kept,

He traced the sound
Mere feet away . . .
That terror drowned.
But on that day

Badge 5-6-9
Did all he could
To redefine
Uncommon good.

Of the more than 2,700 people who died in the World Trade Center attacks of September 11, 2001, 343 of them were firefighters. Those present that day have recalled the sight of firemen charging up smoke-filled staircases of the 110-story buildings that most others were struggling to descend. This is just one example of the firefighter's daily heroism.

THE NUN

Sister Jeannette Normandin
Ruah Assisted Living Center
Cambridge, Massachusetts

I find them living on the street
In homeless shelters, mental wards,
Around the corner from defeat.
What future are they moving towards?

Life is a pocketful of things
To women who live—and die—with AIDS.
And what a little comfort brings
Is nothing next to great crusades.

But I meet women who will be
Like them, alone and deathly ill.
I'm what they know of family.
Life is a pocketful to fill.

In 1994 Sister Jeannette Normandin founded
Ruah, an assisted living center for women with
AIDS. There she has successfully steered some of
her charges away from prison, offering comfort and
acceptance when others looked away. The center
has become a model of tolerance and care for the
terminally ill.

THE GREAT ONE

Roberto Clemente
Pittsburgh Pirates Right Fielder, 1934–1972

Traveling over Roberto Clemente Bridge
One thinks of the man and his important positions:
President of a small patch called right field,
Unofficial Ambassador to Home Plate,
Emperor of Extra Bases, Owner of the Rifle Arm,
Roberto became another name for perfection.
Three thousand hits, twelve Gold Gloves, the Hall
Of Fame. But he saved his greatest heroics to
Rescue earthquake victims of Nicaragua.
Immediately after takeoff, his DC-7 relief plane
Crashed at sea. And so was written regret
On an otherwise festive New Year's Eve, 1972.

The first Latino inducted into the Baseball Hall of Fame, Roberto Clemente was also a dedicated humanitarian. He died in a plane crash while bringing supplies to earthquake victims in South America.

THE BAREBACK RIDER

Lady Godiva
Tax Protestor
England, A.D. mid to late eleventh century

Do you remember me? I rode
Through crowds in Coventry astride
My horse one day with nothing on—
It was a very famous ride.

I told my husband, Leofric,
If he would only help the poor
By cutting taxes, I would give
An in-the-altogether tour.

And so I paced the marketplace
Naked and proud for all to see
Enlightenment in this corner
Of the eleventh century.

Nine hundred years ago, Lady Godiva's husband, the Earl of Mercia, had ambitious build-ing plans that he intended to finance by raising taxes. But Lady G., afraid that high taxes would be too difficult for the poorest citizens to pay, made her husband promise that if she would ride nude on horseback through the center of town, he would accept a more modest increase in taxes.

THE PREACHERS

Martin Luther King Jr. and Mahalia Jackson
The Civil Rights March, August 28, 1963
Washington, D.C.

Thousands of people heard
The man awake the sun.
His morning-glory word
Would dawn on Washington.

I have a Dream. Rejoice!
Then Mahalia swelled the stage.
Sweet thunder in the voice,
Black lightning on his page.

A nation held its breath.
His words not heard before
Made Martin's life—and death—
A freedom metaphor.

The Queen of Gospel wrung
From every blessed bar
Pure grace-notes that she sung,
And flung them very far.

At the 1963 Civil Rights march in
Washington, D.C., Dr. Martin Luther
King Jr. gave his famous "I Have a Dream"
speech, which continues to inspire people to
work towards a more just society. Mahalia
Jackson preceded that speech with the spiritual
"I Been 'Buked and I Been Scorned." She also
sang at Reverend King's funeral.

THE ORGANIZER

Cesar Chavez
Migrant Labor Organizer, 1927–1993

Cesar was a peaceable fighter
With his back against the wall.
He was the David to Goliaths,
One worker against them all.

Up from the Mexican culture,
He rallied migrants to unite
And challenged consumers to boycott
Five years for the grape pickers' plight.

Cesar won and lost many battles
But never resorted to arms,
And carried the torch for *La Causa*
Across California farms.

Poor migrants, whose harvest was hunger,
Depended on him to be strong,
To ignite the fight and fight for right
And everywhere right the wrong.

Mexican-American Cesar Chavez is an enduring symbol of nonviolence and reform. Jailed repeatedly for his beliefs, he successfully brought national attention to the plight of migrant workers.

THE RIVETER

"Rosie the Riveter,"
nickname for all women working in
American wartime industries
1941–1945

"Liberty" ships
And "Victory" ships,
Built mid the factory's roar,
When America ran
Without the man
Who was off to fight the war.

Mothers and grannies pitched in hard—
Factory, foundry, shipping yard—
Rivets and bolts, hammers and drills
Humming to the hum of the lumber mills.

High I beams
And welders' seams
Making *His*tory with a *Her.*
They staked their claim
To the famous name
Of Rosie the Riveter.

In the 1940's over 6 million women from all backgrounds, and from every corner of the country,
went to work in factories to help build tanks, planes, and other equipment needed to fight World
War II. Immortalized in the 1942 song "Rosie the Riveter," the nickname stuck.

THE JOURNALIST

Ida Wells-Barnett
1862–1931

What stuck like a stone
In the soreness of her heart
Was the celebration of evil
In the mob's savage laughter.

Challenging white injustice,
Ida Wells wrote under threat
Without fear, shining a black light
On the barbarity of lynching.

Three of her friends, Memphis
Owners of People's Grocery,
Were lynched for daring to peddle
Greens in white neighborhoods.

What is a hanging, she asked,
If not a crime beyond forgiving?
What is a lynching if not morality
Strangled at the end of a rope?

The daughter of slaves, Ida Wells-Barnett wrote newspaper articles and gave speeches that comprised a crusade against the practice of lynching. She was also one of the founding members of the National Association for the Advancement of Colored People (NAACP).

THE SOLDIER

Joan of Arc
France, 1412–1431

Joan had a very strange career.
She fought the English without fear

Because, she said, the hand of God
Had made her France's lightning rod.

Before they called her Saint (much later),
They called her Witch, Wench, Agitator

And burned the soldier at the stake—
An innocent, for heaven's sake.

At age twelve, Joan heard the voices of saints instruct her to take up arms against the invaders. Disguised as a man, she commanded French troops during the Hundred Years War against England. Though her forces won miraculous battles, Joan was later captured and sold to the English. Burned at the stake in 1431 for charges of witchcraft, she is the patron saint of the French and their national she-ro.

THE STEADFAST

Rosa Parks
Civil Rights Activist
b. 1913

Today it seems preposterous—
Freedom forged inside a bus!

So much was riding down that street—
One fare, one passenger, one seat.
One black woman who would not retreat

When her Montgomery ride awoke
The 1955 white folk,
Who sent the city up in smoke.

Which fellow was your fellow man?
Not Jim Crow nor the Ku Klux Klan.
The fight for civil rights began.

And she who sat against the tide
Stood up for Justice nationwide.

On her way home from work Rosa Parks boarded a Montgomery, Alabama, city bus but refused to move to the back, as the law required all blacks to do in the segregated South of 1955. Her defiant act helped inspire a nearly yearlong bus boycott and sparked the revolution called the Civil Rights Movement.

THE IMMIGRANTS

No house was built of silver,
No streets were paved with gold,
None would forget
The summer sweat
Or the winters bitter cold.

The language was a mouthful,
The culture seemed so strange.
They gave their best
To the rugged test—
To make a foreign exchange.

To transform this new nation,
They opened up closed doors
And bravely rolled
New into old
To cultivate these shores.

*"Give me your tired, your poor, your huddled masses yearning
to breathe free," wrote Emma Lazarus of the millions of
immigrants streaming into America. With tenacity, creativity,
and grit, immigrants brought their Old World ways and
values to every corner of their new country—and changed
America forever, both then and now.*

THE CHILD LABORER

Iqbal Masih
Pakistan, 1982–1995

Iqbal Masih—Pakistan.
Father sold him to a man.
Sixteen dollars, the going price.
Five-year-olds were merchandise.
The factory owner—dealer in doom—
Chained him to a carpet loom.
Slaving long hours without food,
Iqbal found the fortitude
To escape an inhumane
Never-ending house of pain.

Men occasionally destroy
Youth and spirit, but the boy,
Ten years old, led a crusade—
Life, the highest price he paid—
Against some of the greatest crimes
Perpetrated in modern times.

A Pakistani boy, Iqbal Masih, was one of the warriors in the long, painful struggle to end the debt enslavement of children. Taken young, Iqbal escaped after five years of servitude. At great risk he went on to gather evidence and became an international crusader for child workers worldwide. He was shot and killed at age twelve by unknown assailants.

So heroes set aside their fear
To lend a hand or lend an ear,

To face the night or save the day
And never look the other way.

They do not, with a single bound,
Leap up tall buildings from the ground.

But from a sense of decency,
They share themselves with you and me.

No matter what or where or who,
When something must be done,
They do.

Author's Note

My first hero was Nate Landrum, our school janitor. To me he was in some ways rather mysterious. For one thing, he was the first African-American I ever knew. And though I didn't realize it then, I think the kind of person he was shaped how I thought about race for the rest of my life. As a kid I always wondered what his life was like, where he lived, where his rusty Pontiac Chieftain took him at the end of every day. But I never found out.

What I did know was that Nate Landrum made life better for everyone he met at St. Mary of the Lake School. Not only did he work hard to make our old school sparkle, Nate Landrum was a peacemaker. You couldn't be mad or sad or nasty when he was around. *Wanna see my submarine powered by baking soda?* he'd ask a bully. *Did you know dogs can hear a whistle humans can't?* he'd tell an upset second-grader. Then he'd pull out the whistle, blow on it, wait to hear a dog bark, and share that whistle like you were the only person in the whole world he would even *think* of letting in on the secret. Just talking to him made you grow a foot and a half in your dreams.

Nate Landrum always put other people first. What else could you hope for in a hero?

Though I hope some of the other kids from my school remember and appreciate Mr. Landrum, he'll never really be famous. Some heroes, like Abraham Lincoln, Anne Frank, Harriet Tubman, and Nelson Mandela, are famous, but, like Mr. Landrum, it is the good they did on behalf of others that makes them heroes.

What it takes to be a hero,
from beginning to end
Is exactly what it takes
to be the truest friend.